MW00966408

RONA MUNRO

Rona Munro has written extensively for stage, radio, film and television including the award-winning plays *Iron* (Traverse Theatre and Royal Court, London), *Bold Girls* (7:84 and Hampstead Theatre) and *The Maiden Stone* (Hampstead Theatre).

Other credits include *The Last Witch* for the Traverse Theatre and the Edinburgh International Festival, *Long Time Dead* for Paines Plough and the Drum Theatre Plymouth, *The Indian Boy* and *Little Eagles* for the Royal Shakespeare Company, *Pandas* for the Traverse in Edinburgh and *The James Plays* for the National Theatre of Scotland, the Edinburgh International Festival and the National Theatre of Great Britain. She is the co-founder, with actress Fiona Knowles, of Scotland's oldest continuously performing, small-scale touring theatre company, The Msfits. Their one-woman shows have toured every year since 1986.

Film and television work includes the Ken Loach film *Ladybird Ladybird*, *Aimee and Jaguar* and television dramas *Rehab* (directed by Antonia Bird) and BAFTA-nominated *Bumping the Odds* for the BBC. She has also written many other single plays for television and contributed to series including *Casualty* and *Dr Who*. Most recently, she wrote the screenplay for *Oranges and Sunshine*, directed by Jim Loach and starring Emily Watson and Hugo Weaving.

She has contributed several radio plays to the Stanley Baxter Playhouse series on BBC Radio 4.

Other Titles in this Series

Mike Bartlett
BULL
AN INTERVENTION
KING CHARLES III

Jez Butterworth
JERUSALEM
JEZ BUTTERWORTH PLAYS: ONE
MOJO
THE NIGHT HERON
PARLOUR SONG
THE RIVER
THE WINTERLING

Caryl Churchill
BLUE HEART
CHURCHILL PLAYS: THREE
CHURCHILL PLAYS: FOUR
CHURCHILL: SHORTS
CLOUD NINE
DING DONG THE WICKED
A DREAM PLAY
    after Strindberg
DRUNK ENOUGH TO SAY
    I LOVE YOU?
FAR AWAY
HOTEL
ICECREAM
LIGHT SHINING IN
    BUCKINGHAMSHIRE
LOVE AND INFORMATION
MAD FOREST
A NUMBER
SEVEN JEWISH CHILDREN
THE SKRIKER
THIS IS A CHAIR
THYESTES *after* Seneca
TRAPS

Stella Feehily
BANG BANG BANG
DREAMS OF VIOLENCE
DUCK
O GO MY MAN
THIS MAY HURT A BIT

Vivienne Franzmann
MOGADISHU
PESTS
THE WITNESS

debbie tucker green
BORN BAD
DIRTY BUTTERFLY
NUT
RANDOM
STONING MARY
TRADE & GENERATIONS
TRUTH AND RECONCILIATION

Vicky Jones
THE ONE

Lucy Kirkwood
BEAUTY AND THE BEAST
    with Katie Mitchell
BLOODY WIMMIN
CHIMERICA
HEDDA *after* Ibsen
IT FELT EMPTY WHEN THE
    HEART WENT AT FIRST BUT
    IT IS ALRIGHT NOW
NSFW
TINDERBOX

Liz Lochhead
BLOOD AND ICE
DRACULA *after* Stoker
EDUCATING AGNES ('The School
    for Wives') *after* Molière
GOOD THINGS
LIZ LOCHHEAD: FIVE PLAYS
MARY QUEEN OF SCOTS GOT
    HER HEAD CHOPPED OFF
MEDEA *after* Euripides
MISERYGUTS ('The Miser')
    & TARTUFFE *after* Molière
PERFECT DAYS
THEBANS *after* Euripides & Sophocles

Linda McLean
ANY GIVEN DAY
ONE GOOD BEATING
RIDDANCE
SHIMMER
STRANGERS, BABIES

Conor McPherson
DUBLIN CAROL
McPHERSON PLAYS: ONE
McPHERSON PLAYS: TWO
McPHERSON PLAYS: THREE
THE NIGHT ALIVE
PORT AUTHORITY
THE SEAFARER
SHINING CITY
THE VEIL
THE WEIR

Rona Munro
THE ASTRONAUT'S CHAIR
THE HOUSE OF BERNARDA ALBA
    after Lorca
THE INDIAN BOY
IRON
THE JAMES PLAYS
LITTLE EAGLES
LONG TIME DEAD
THE MAIDEN STONE
MARY BARTON *after* Gaskell
PANDAS
STRAWBERRIES IN JANUARY
    from de la Chenelière
YOUR TURN TO CLEAN THE STAIR
    & FUGUE

Rona Munro

THE LAST WITCH

NICK HERN BOOKS

London

www.nickhernbooks.co.uk

A Nick Hern Book

The Last Witch first published in 2009 by Nick Hern Books Limited, The Glasshouse, 49a Goldhawk Road, London W12 8QP

Reprinted 2010, 2011, 2014

The Last Witch copyright © 2009 Rona Munro

Rona Munro has asserted her right to be identified as the author of this work

Cover image © Linda Plaisted
Cover designed by Ned Hoste

Typeset by Nick Hern Books, London
Printed in the UK by CPI Group (UK) Ltd

A CIP catalogue record for this book is available from the British Library

ISBN   978 1 84842 072 4

CAUTION   All rights whatsoever in this play are strictly reserved. Requests to reproduce the text in whole or in part should be addressed to the publisher.

Amateur Performing Rights   Applications for performance, including readings and excerpts, by amateurs in the English language throughout the world should be addressed to the Performing Rights Manager, Nick Hern Books, The Glasshouse, 49a Goldhawk Road, London W12 8QP, *tel* +44 (0)20 8749 4953, *e-mail* info@nickhernbooks.co.uk, except as follows:

Australia: Dominie Drama, 8 Cross Street, Brookvale 2100, *fax* (2) 9938 8695, *e-mail* drama@dominie.com.au

New Zealand: Play Bureau, PO Box 9013, St Clair, Dunedin 9047, *tel* (3) 455 9959, *e-mail* play.bureau.nz@xtra.co.nzz

South Africa: DALRO (pty) Ltd, PO Box 31627, 2017 Braamfontein, *tel* (11) 712 8000, *fax* (11) 403 9094, *e-mail* theatricals@dalro.co.za

United States of America and Canada: Independent Talent Group Ltd, see details below

Professional Performing Rights   Applications for performance by professionals in any medium and in any language throughout the world (and amateur and stock performances in the United States of America and Canada) should be addressed to Independent Talent Group Ltd, 40 Whitfield Street, London W1T 2RH, *tel* +44 (020) 7636 6565

No performance of any kind may be given unless a licence has been obtained. Applications should be made before rehearsals begin. Publication of this play does not necessarily indicate their availability for amateur performance.

The Last Witch was commissioned by Edinburgh International Festival and co-produced by the Festival and the Traverse Theatre Company. It opened at the Royal Lyceum Theatre, Edinburgh, on 23 August 2009, with the following cast:

JANET HORNE	Kathryn Howden
HELEN HORNE	Hannah Donaldson
DOUGLAS BEGG	George Anton
ELSPETH BEGG	Vicki Liddelle
NIALL	Neil McKinven
CAPTAIN DAVID ROSS	Andy Clark
NICK	Ryan Fletcher
HARPSICHORD	Simon Smith

Director Dominic Hill
Designer Naomi Wilkinson
Lighting Designer Chris Davey
Composer and Sound Designer John Harris
Video Designer Andrzej Goulding
Choreographer Kally Lloyd Jones
Dramaturg Katherine Mendelsohn

Characters

JANET HORNE
HELEN HORNE
DOUGLAS BEGG
ELSPETH BEGG
NIALL, *a minister*
CAPTAIN DAVID ROSS, *the sheriff*
NICK

This text went to press before the end of rehearsals and so may differ slightly from the play as performed.

ACT ONE

Scene One

Near Janet Horne's house – a midsummer afternoon.

The house overlooks the hill behind and the shore below.

It is a warm summer afternoon, a rare northern treat.

JANET *is standing soaking in the sun, her face turned up to the sky, muttering to herself.* HELEN, *her daughter, enters, she watches her mother for a while.*

HELEN. Mother?

 JANET *goes on muttering.*

 Mother, what are you doing?

 JANET *stops. Looks at her daughter in exasperation.*

JANET. Why can't I be a crow?

HELEN. Mother, there's no peat in the stack.

JANET. Why not? The charm's easy to see, to imagine.

 She looks at the sky, raises her arms.

 (*This is what she's been muttering.*) Make my fingers black, make my bones grow to thin feathers, let me rustle and shine with dark-blue, oily light. Crumple me into a pinioned, prickling ball and throw me up onto the wind!

HELEN. The fire's out!

JANET. Oh, of course it is!

 Of course it is.

 Staring up into the clouds a moment longer.

 And the wind is sulking in some cavern in the sky. It won't come out for all my calling.

Bad dog.   *devil?*

Bad, bad, bad, bad dog.

HELEN (*quiet*). You can't call the wind.

JANET. What are you talking about? You've seen me do it. A hundred times.

HELEN. Once.

JANET. A score of times. What's the matter with you?

HELEN *says nothing*.

There was something in the air today. A warmer air. Reminding me of what I could be. I thought to raise a hot wind and fly upon it.

HELEN. I'd like to see that. I've never seen you fly.

JANET. Nor will you. You decided to fix your eyes on the ground the first time you stood up and you've scarce looked up since. Have you?

I'm surprised you know the sky's above you. You don't look up even when it's raining on your head.

HELEN. I watch the sky.

JANET. And can you fly in it? No. You've a head full of dry beans and a voice full of moaning like a wet wind.

(*Imitating.*) 'There's no peat, there's no bread, there's stones in my bed…'

If I hadn't pulled your head out of my own body I'd doubt you were mine.

A beat.

HELEN. I don't think you've ever flown.

JANET. Well, you would think that.

HELEN. Why?

JANET. Because I'm your mother. I can do the great magic… I just need to remember… another wind…

She's searching the air with her fingers.

HELEN. Make me pretty, then.

JANET. Mary MacKenzie believes in me. I cured her pig. You can't deny that pig's grunting happier since I put my hand on it.

HELEN. Make me beautiful.

JANET. You are beautiful.

HELEN. To you. What use is that?

Make us a fire and a pot of soup to hang on it.

JANET. That's your job.

HELEN. There's no peat in the stack!

JANET. Who's stolen our peat?!

HELEN. I don't know. Someone. There was scarce a crumb of mud left anyway.

JANET. I'll charm the truth out and then I'll curse them. That peat'll burn so dark and drear the smoke'll shrivel their lungs.

HELEN. No you won't.

JANET. What's the matter with you today?!

A beat.

HELEN. What are we going to eat?

JANET. Honeycomb.

HELEN. Oh aye? And where are we finding that?

JANET (*unconvinced*). I'm going to become a bee.

A beat. They look together over the hills, the distant sea.

Why are you so restless?

HELEN. I'm hot.

A beat.

William Mackenzie wants me to sit in his cart when we go to the peats.

JANET. Ah! And here's the matter. I've told you.

You're not for William Mackenzie.

HELEN. Why not?

JANET. Until you've the sense to know that, you're not fit to be let out of my sight. You'll stay here till you learn you're not fit for anyone within a hundred miles of here.

HELEN. So what will I do then? When I've learned that?

JANET. You can't learn that. Look at you, bursting out your dress but still rooted here like a bush of gorse... Can't put your hand on it, can't dig it up...

A beat.

Can you hear them? Droning in the heather bells.

HELEN. It will be months before we go to cut the peats again anyway.

JANET. I can hear them. I can see them shimmering in thousands over the hill...

HELEN. You don't know how it is at the peats. We'd have no fire all winter if the Beggs didn't take me to cut it. I cut our warmth. *I* travel out under a sky full of ice.

JANET. Silver wings. Peppery little bodies full of sharp sting. I can feel what a bee is all right.

HELEN. I didn't close my eyes all night. There was someone singing in the darkness behind me. I looked up at the stars and there were different hilltops between me and their sparkle.

JANET. Mouths like little black straws, sucking the sweet heart of every flower. I can taste it.

HELEN. I was somewhere else. I was on the other side of the hills. Cutting peat in the cold morning and bringing it home. Two days under another piece of sky.

JANET. Shatter myself into a thousand sweet buzzing pieces. Make me a swarm of bees.

HELEN *holds out a little silver knife.*

HELEN. I cut this out of the darkest earth, damp, black soil, crumbling with sleeping fire. I found silver. It might be fairy silver buried in the hill, I found it... Look...

JANET *doesn't even hear her, murmuring to the sky.*

(*Putting the knife away.*) Fine then. You'll never know what I have. I shan't tell you. Ever.

JANET. Nothing.

The words aren't the charm. The words don't make it happen.

HELEN. William doesn't mind my hands...

JANET. Mind!? Why should he mind!?

All he's thinking is they work well enough to push a hoe! If he saw you as you should be seen he'd never be thinking about your hands at all! Why are you so stupid you'll never learn that!? God, I wish I'd never dropped you out at all! Keeping me here, stuck in mud that can't even grow weeds with no one to talk to but rocks and a daughter that's stupider than a lump of cow shite!

A moment. HELEN is too upset to answer. JANET softens at once.

Oh... my tongue's straight off the whetstone. I didn't mean it, pet. Come here.

JANET *puts her arms round HELEN. HELEN lets herself be comforted.*

I'm sorry.

HELEN. All right.

JANET. Elspeth Begg only loves you because she lost her own daughter. You know that?

HELEN. You told me.

JANET. Now there's a careless mother. Grows a girl and can't keep her. And she casts her eyes at me because I can't keep chickens.

A beat.

Well… it's a bonny day. There's that.

HELEN. Yes.

JANET. We'll have no need of a fire tonight.

HELEN. No.

JANET. Elspeth will let us have a basket of peat.

HELEN. She always does.

They've settled close together, looking out over the day.

It would frighten me.

JANET. What would?

HELEN. If you were just bees.

JANET. I'd come back again. I'll always come back.

(*As* HELEN *says nothing.*) Why wouldn't I come back?

HELEN. Because you know the way to far away.

JANET *leans in to her. She lifts* HELEN*'s twisted hands, stroking them.*

JANET. And you never will, pet. But I'll stay here and polish you. My beautiful stone.

DOUGLAS BEGG *enters. He is in a quiet rage, ready to boil over.*

DOUGLAS. Take it off.

JANET. Good afternoon, Mr Begg.

DOUGLAS. Take the curse off.

JANET. It's a lovely afternoon. How are all under your roof?

DOUGLAS. I'm warning you, Mistress Horne…

JANET. We are all well, thank you, as you see…

DOUGLAS. Take it off!

JANET. Only wanting a few sods of peat.

A beat.

DOUGLAS. They weren't yours.

JANET. What weren't?

DOUGLAS. Elspeth let the girl cut them from our side of the hill. I took back what was mine.

JANET. Douglas Begg. Did you steal our peat?

DOUGLAS. It was not stealing!

JANET. You dared to take my peat!

DOUGLAS. Put your hand down! You've cursed me already!

HELEN (*under this*). Her hand's not up.

JANET. There's worse than that coming to you! There's worse than that! Oh, you'll fear me now!

DOUGLAS. I'm in the right of it! You took my peat, you starved my cattle…

JANET. I've not been near your beasts! I'll starve them now! I'll see them lying like piles of black sticks on dead grass… The Deil'll dance in your byre, Douglas Begg!

DOUGLAS. Take it back!

Under this, ELSPETH *is entering with a great heavy basket of peats on her back.*

Take it back or I'll tear the thatch off your roof and burn it in front of your eyes!

JANET. And you do, your own eyes will melt out your head and run down your face like stinking tallow!

DOUGLAS. You'll threaten me no more!

HELEN *is helping* ELSPETH *take the basket of peats off her back.*

JANET. The heart'll burst out of your chest and run in flames before you down the road.

DOUGLAS. It's you that's the black heart! I'll not fear you!

JANET. You'll fear me! Every beast, every human soul that's yours will know the weight of my cursing!

ELSPETH. Good afternoon to you, Mistress Horne.

JANET. Mistress Begg.

ELSPETH. My husband took this peat of yours by mistake and I've brought it back. We're very sorry for your trouble.

JANET. Are you now?

ELSPETH. We are. The both of us. Very sorry.

JANET (*looking at* DOUGLAS). The both of you?

A beat.

DOUGLAS. Take the sickness off my beasts. That's all I ask.

JANET. I hear you asking.

ELSPETH. I've brought a jug of milk and a cloth of oatcakes, Janet.

JANET. Aw, Elspeth, that's good of you.

HELEN. We've no soup made.

JANET. Having no fire.

All the women are now looking expectantly at DOUGLAS. *He struggles for a moment.*

DOUGLAS. Well then… I'm sorry for it.

DOUGLAS *exits.*

JANET *gives a bark of laughter.*

JANET. Oh, you're sorry now.

ELSPETH *is laying out the oatcakes on a cloth.*

ELSPETH. There's a wee bit cheese as well. We'll eat together.

HELEN. Cheese!

ELSPETH. Just a crumb.

JANET. We'll not take your last crumb of cheese, Elspeth.

ELSPETH. We'll share it. Better so.

JANET. No, no. It's for you. It's for market. Milk's enough.

HELEN. Aw, but cheese…

> ELSPETH *has put a little bit of cheese on an oatcake. She holds it out to* JANET.

ELSPETH. Here.

> JANET *takes it.*

Eat now, and so will I.

> HELEN *half-reaches out, desperate for her share.*

> *The other two women eat.*

JANET. It's good cheese, Elspeth. Thank you.

ELSPETH. So. All's well between us now?

> *Both women pass their half-eaten oatcakes and cheese to* HELEN, *who falls on them.* ELSPETH *is passing round the milk.*

JANET. Elspeth Begg, are you afraid of me?

ELSPETH. Three cows are shaking on their legs, Janet. Their eyes are halfway back in their heads. I don't like to see a beast suffer so.

> *A beat.*

JANET. Well… it wasn't what I wanted.

ELSPETH. It's a black shame.

JANET. So what else have you to say?

ELSPETH. Is the milk good? You're happy to share the jug with me?

JANET. My mouth where yours has been and no ill will
between us.

ELSPETH. He was in the right.

JANET. When?

ELSPETH. When he stopped you cutting the hay in our
meadow.

JANET. Oh, it was your meadow, was it…?

ELSPETH (*cutting over her*). As far as the oak trees is ours,
Janet! There's no wall, no stones to keep you out, nothing to
stop you but use and custom and the trust between us, but
you know that, you know it, you know it. And we've beasts
to feed through winter when all you're after is meadow
flowers sweet in your mattress. You'd no business cutting
our winter hay!

A beat.

JANET. He dared me to it.

I was nowhere near. I was cutting way over by the burn. He
called over and warned me not to flick the blade on anything
of his. The thought wasn't even in my head till he put it there.

ELSPETH. He's a slow tongue but every word's a stone he's
throwing at somebody.

A beat.

He drives me to red rage but my words fall on his back and
on his head like drizzle and fog. He scarce bothers to turn up
his collar to ward me off.

That's how…

Well. You know my sorrow.

A beat.

Is it the feed? Have you cursed the grass in the fields? Must
we pasture them elsewhere?

JANET. Just till it rains.

Walk them further up the burn to water them.

ELSPETH. I'll do that.

I don't grudge you the cheese, Janet, but I wish you'd think harder about who your anger hurts.

JANET. And if I'd raised my hand that day in the meadow, spared the beasts and turned him into a twisted thorn...?

ELSPETH. Well...

Maybe I need a good thorn stick to drive those beasts up the hill.

All the women crack up laughing.

As long as I don't lose another milker.

JANET. We're glad of the milk.

ELSPETH. It's no bother.

A beat.

JANET. Sometimes... sometimes I don't know myself what'll happen when the cursing starts.

ELSPETH. That's your burden then.

HELEN (*quiet*). Nothing so bad ever happens.

A beat.

JANET *looks at* HELEN.

JANET. She doubts me today, Elspeth.

ELSPETH. She does? Why's that?

JANET. Likely it's her age.

ELSPETH. Well... it would be past time.

(*To* HELEN.) Never doubt your mother, Helen. She's a powerful woman.

(*To* JANET.) Something I've always wanted to ask you...

She hesitates.

JANET. So ask me.

ELSPETH (*half-laughing*). I can't.

JANET. No, go on.

ELSPETH. When you see him…

JANET. Who?

ELSPETH. The… (*Can't go on, giggling*.) Oh, see, I can't…!

JANET. Elspeth!

HELEN. Tell us!

ELSPETH. When you see the… Devil…

JANET. Oh, him.

ELSPETH. What does he look like?

JANET. Och, he's the spit of Alexander Ross's cattle man.

ELSPETH. Is he!?

JANET. Not so fat but… same nose.

> ELSPETH *is gaping at her, totally credulous.* JANET *cracks up.*

> I've never met the Devil, Elspeth.

ELSPETH. Have you not?

JANET. Why would I!?

ELSPETH. But is that not… Is that not how you…? Does he not help you do all you do?

JANET. No one helps me. Helen and me live alone.

ELSPETH. So how…?

JANET. I am on this road… see… walking dark lands, seeing wonders… The Devil's beside me in the darkness… Maybe I smell him… maybe I hear his hooves on the black stones of that road… maybe sometimes his breath is on my neck… but I find my own way through that country.

ELSPETH. Oh, I'd be feart for that! Oh! His hot breath on your neck!

JANET. Cold. Everything about the Devil is icy cold. His breath, his touch. His cock's an icicle.

HELEN. How do you know that?

JANET. Everyone knows that.

ELSPETH. So you wouldn't...

JANET. What?

ELSPETH. You wouldn't lie with the Devil?

JANET. I wouldn't lie with any male thing that didn't woo me first. The Devil's too good an idea of himself if you ask me.

HELEN. But he could give you anything. He could give you gold. He could... turn you into a bird...

JANET. If it suited him.

HELEN. Could you call him? Could you call up the Devil?

JANET. If it suited me.

ELSPETH. Christ save us.

HELEN. How?

A beat.

JANET. Oh, she doubts me yet? You know not to ask me these things, Helen.

HELEN. Elspeth wants to know.

A beat.

JANET. I could never step in a church again if I did it.

ELSPETH. Oh, save us.

HELEN. Do you know the words to say then? Really?

A beat.

JANET. Stand under a full moon. Look up at the sky... Say, 'I will have no master but you...' Ask him to come to you.

ELSPETH. And he'd come?

JANET. Like a stag to the hind. Stepping out of the forest in all his cold pride.

A beat.

HELEN. And you'd never know want again.

JANET. So they say.

A beat.

ELSPETH. You've never thought to call him?

JANET. We want for nothing. You bring us oatcakes and milk.

ELSPETH (*getting up*). Oh aye. Aye, I'll do that yet.

ELSPETH *gathers up her things,* HELEN *helps her.*

He'll likely still speak at the kirk session, Janet. His anger's like damp peat. Gives you no good but black smoke, but it burns for days.

JANET. Oh, I'm tired of this!

ELSPETH. Well… I'm sorry for it… But he's who he is.

JANET. It's you I'm sorry for.

ELSPETH. I've oatcakes and cheese, Janet. And two rooms to my house. You've not even a chimney to yours.

JANET. There's that.

ELSPETH. A good day, then.

JANET. A good day.

ELSPETH *exits.*

A beat.

The sun'll be a long time setting tonight.

HELEN. There's cockle-pickers on the shore. Look.

JANET. Best put a lock on the outhouse tonight.

HELEN. You could walk on that water.

JANET. Walk to France.

HELEN. Is that straight out there?

JANET. No. No. Look to the south. Look to the south.

Why are you so restless, Helen?

HELEN. I don't know.

JANET. If the travellers are coming through we'll get you ribbons.

HELEN. We've no coins.

JANET. I'll charm them.

A beat.

HELEN. You didn't know the Beggs' cows were sick, did you?

JANET *says nothing.*

Did you curse him?

JANET. I'd not thought of it. Maybe I sensed his treachery in my sleep. It's true. Even my dreaming would have the power to curse him.

HELEN. So did you?

JANET. You can see that I did.

HELEN. I've never seen you work any charm as powerful as that.

JANET. And now you have.

A beat.

We've work to get on with. Floors need swept, pease need ground. I'll fetch the water.

HELEN. It's evening already.

JANET. While there's light, we can work.

JANET exits. After a moment, HELEN follows.

Scene Two

Near the cathedral in Dornoch – early evening.

NIALL, *the minister, and* CAPTAIN DAVID ROSS, *the sheriff, are talking in the empty market grounds near the half-ruined cathedral.*

NIALL. There… where the grass is greener.

    ROSS *sees the place he indicates. He bends to examine it.*

ROSS. She cursed this spot?

NIALL. So they say.

ROSS. Why?

NIALL. It was a winter market day. One of the other women had lit a fire with some rubbish. The sparks flew into Mistress Horne's cloak.

ROSS. And she cursed the fire.

NIALL. Yes.

ROSS. And now no flame will burn here?

NIALL. Yes.

ROSS. No fire will burn or no one cares to light one?

NIALL. I don't know. You can see how bright the grass is there.

ROSS. Charcoal will feed grass roots.

NIALL (*smiling in agreement*). Exactly, but… well… there it is. Green. 'The Devil's colour.' That's the talk so…

ROSS (*interrupting*). She's a known witch?

    NIALL *is suddenly uncomfortable.*

    You're bringing me the complaint. You want me to proceed against her as a witch.

NIALL. No one has made such a complaint for… I can't remember such a complaint.

ROSS. Well... the law's clear enough.

NIALL. No one has made such a complaint to the kirk session
in all my years here.

ROSS. Is Douglas Begg a man of good character?

NIALL. Yes, yes... but...

ROSS. And the woman?

NIALL. Janet Horne. She's neighbour to the Beggs. In Loth.

ROSS. Married?

NIALL. Widowed. She has a daughter, fully grown now. Helen.

Helen has... her hands and feet... are twisted.

ROSS. She's deformed.

NIALL. No, no! She's pretty, a pretty, bright girl but her fingers
are... it's something like a claw...

ROSS. A claw?

NIALL. You don't see it until she tries to pick up something
small... really, she's a lovely girl.

ROSS *pokes at the grass a bit more.*

ROSS. Are you asking me to take this case further?

NIALL. Well, I had to tell you about it.

Douglas Begg is...

He will be easier if he knows we've spoken.

ROSS. And after we've spoken? What should happen then,
minister?

NIALL. Well... that's not... I mean, I couldn't say...

ROSS (*cutting over this*). Because the law is clear.

NIALL. Of course, of course... but she's not... I mean, she's
not really a witch as such just...

NIALL *trails off.* ROSS *waits.*

She has a temper... She has a dirty, hot mouth when she's angry...

She has healed beasts as well as cursed them... but...

ROSS. Under the law, any charm, good or ill, is the Devil's work.

Awkward pause.

NIALL. Perhaps when she first came to Loth... there was some talk... but no one talks about that any more.

ROSS. We're talking about it now.

Have you ever seen a witch, minister?

NIALL. No.

ROSS. I have.

NIALL *waits but* ROSS *says nothing more.*

NIALL. I don't think Janet Horne has any harm in her.

ROSS. When she first came to Loth... there was talk?

NIALL. Yes, I believe... I've been told...

ROSS. She came from where?

NIALL. Oh, she knew her husband's family... she was only born on the other side of Sutherland, I believe. But she'd lately been a ladies' maid in Italy...

ROSS. Italy!?

NIALL. Yes.

ROSS. Well... there's some would say the Devil's living in Italy today. lol

A beat.

NIALL. You fought... in the old war?

ROSS. Yes.

NIALL. We're...

ROSS. What?

NIALL (*uncertain*). Honoured?

> A man of your history… in our little parish.

ROSS. Oh, my history's not such a hero's tale.

> And Dornoch's not such a small place…

NIALL. Still…

ROSS (*brisk*). If I serve well here I may serve as well in larger places before I'm done.

> That's the way of it.

> Now. Our business.

NIALL. It is just talk, sheriff… and Douglas Begg… when he gets an idea in his head it sticks like tar on wool…

> (*Brisk.*) So. So we've talked of it now. I can tell the kirk session it's all been reported…

ROSS. I'll decide what further action's needed once I've talked to the woman.

> *A beat.*

NIALL. You're going to talk to her.

ROSS. She must be interviewed.

NIALL. Yes. Indeed. Of course.

> Should I come?

ROSS. That's entirely up to yourself, minister.

NIALL. I think I should come, I know Mistress Horne so…

ROSS. She attends church?

NIALL. Oh yes… yes… Not every Sunday, but… Yes, I know them both.

ROSS. Then come and welcome.

> Church and state, eh? We'll go together. I'll call for you.

NIALL (*hesitates*). All right...

> ROSS *is looking round.*

ROSS. A warm night. It'll be another harvest moon tonight. So much light in it. I doubt you could still read a book under the open sky at midnight.

> Goodnight to you, minister.

Scene Three

Janet Horne's house – after midnight.

HELEN *walks out and looks up at the sky. She is shaking.*

HELEN. I will...

> *She can't say it. She takes a moment, getting her courage.*

> *She turns her face up to the moon.*

> Devil... Lord Devil... I will have no master but you. Come to me now...

> *She waits. There's nothing.*

> *She waits a beat longer, the wired tension falling out of her as nothing happens.*

> *She turns away. A man steps out of the darkness right behind her and puts his hand over her mouth to stop her scream. This is* NICK.

NICK. Don't scream. Don't. Don't make a sound.

> *After a moment he takes his hand away.*

HELEN. Your hand...

NICK. Yes?

HELEN. It's ice.

NICK. You live here?

HELEN. This is my mother's house.

NICK. Is she inside?

HELEN. No.

You came.

NICK *says nothing*.

I called you and you came.

NICK. You sure it was me you were wanting?

HELEN. No.

NICK. Who were you wanting?

HELEN. The Devil.

NICK *says nothing*.

Is it you?

NICK. Look at me.

She's looking.

What do you see?

HELEN. Is it you?

NICK. Tell me.

HELEN. You look like a man.

NICK. I do.

HELEN. You're breathing… like a living man.

She holds her hand out to his mouth.

But your breath is ice.

NICK. It's a cold night.

HELEN. It's not.

NICK. What business have you with the Devil?

HELEN. I've eaten nothing but oats and a crumb of cheese
since Tuesday.

NICK. So steal a chicken.

HELEN. I'm not a thief.

NICK. Where do you think the Devil gets his gold?

HELEN. Where were you going? When I called you?

NICK. I was walking. Making my way through the dark.

HELEN. Is my mother there? In the dark?

NICK *says nothing.*

She's not in her bed.

NICK. I haven't seen her.

You want your mother?

HELEN. No.

NICK. How old are you?

HELEN. Seventeen.

NICK. Why are you so young?

HELEN. I'm not young. I'm full-grown.

NICK. I can see that.

A beat. NICK *steps towards her.* HELEN *steps back and there's a little silver knife in her hand.*

NICK *stops.*

I won't touch you. Unless you're asking me. Are you asking me?

HELEN *says nothing.* NICK *steps towards her again.*

She tries to stab him. He takes the knife.

So. Ask me for what you do want.

HELEN. I'm not wanting anything.

NICK. It's all right. It's all right, I'll not hurt you. I couldn't.

You want to eat cheese? A chicken?

A beat.

HELEN. No. No, now I know you're here… I just want to see you with my own eyes.

NICK. That's all?

HELEN. That's all.

NICK. Then you've had all you want and there's nothing for me here.

NICK vanishes back into the shadows.

HELEN. No, don't! If I call you again, will you come again?

Nothing. No one.

If I call you again will you come again?

Nothing. Then JANET *walks out of the dark in another direction.*

Where have you been?

JANET. I got us a fish.

She holds out her skirts, shows the fish to HELEN.

I lay on the rocks of the shore. The water was warm as blood. The fish were hanging in the dark cold where the sun had died. I put my hand in and called the fish. They came and played with my fingers with their mouths. I waited till I felt the biggest of them sucking on my pinkie like a babe at the teat. Then I called his name and he jumped out the waves to die happy in my lap.

HELEN. Well… I could have done that.

JANET. Called a fish?

HELEN. Tickled one out of the water.

JANET. Out of the sea? I don't think so.

Shall we sleep or shall we eat him?

HELEN. I'm tired. I want my bed.

JANET. Wrap him in grass first. Keep him cool for tomorrow.

HELEN. I'm tired. I want my bed.

> HELEN *exits*.

JANET (*surprised and irritated*). Well. No ribbons for you, milady.

Scene Four

Janet Horne's house – evening.

ROSS *comes up the road and sits waiting outside, easy on the grass, taking in the view.*

JANET *enters. She's carrying a jug.*

JANET. Good evening.

ROSS. Good evening.

JANET. Another bonny day.

ROSS. They tell me not to get used to them.

JANET. Best not. It's a damp disappointment when it comes.

> *A beat.* ROSS *is completely relaxed.*

> You don't know our Dornoch skies, then?

ROSS. I was born out of sight of the sea.

JANET. And it's still a wonder to you.

ROSS. Isn't it a wonder?

JANET. Always.

> *She settles herself close by him, watching the sea as well.*

ROSS. But I have seen a thousand men, all glinting with steel, run down a dark hill and break… like those waves on the rocks.

JANET. I'm sure that was not a bonny day.

So. I heard the new sheriff might come calling.

ROSS. Captain David Ross.

JANET. And what brings you here, Captain Ross?

ROSS. It may be I'm here to arrest you, Mistress Horne.

JANET. On what charge?

ROSS. That you are a known witch.

A beat.

Do you deny it?

JANET *says nothing.*

You will not deny it?

JANET. Is that all your business here today?

ROSS. Well... it's a bonny view.

JANET. It's worth the climb.

ROSS. What charms can you work? Could you charm me?

JANET. That depends.

ROSS. On what?

JANET. On whether you care to be charmed.

ROSS. And if I do?

JANET. I could charm the clothes off your back, Captain Ross.

ROSS. I'll bet you could.

JANET *lifts her jug.*

JANET. I have no bread but the water from the burn is cold.

ROSS. I'll not trouble you. Thank you.

JANET. Would you not drink from my hand?

ROSS. I would not.

JANET. I could take offence at that if I'd a mind to.

ROSS. I'll risk it.

JANET. So you fear me so much?

ROSS. Not your anger.

JANET. My anger is a powerful thing, Captain Ross.

ROSS. I don't doubt it.

JANET. What will protect you?

ROSS. My mother told me I'd a smile that could charm any woman.

JANET laughs.

JANET. Your mother knew her son.

ROSS. So she did.

They smile at each other.

I have never been to Italy. France. France I know, and a little time in the low country.

JANET. In the summer there you can wake in the night... and put your hand on a stone in the wall, a boulder with its roots in the deep earth... and they will still be warm. The deep heart of the earth is always warm. Here... feel the stone...

He does so.

No matter what heat's in the sun here... it's still a cold-hearted land.

ROSS. I like it here. In France there are so many flies that bite you.

JANET. That's true, I'll give you that. But one Dornoch cleg can hurt you worse than all the flies in Europe.

ROSS. They say the Devil takes the form of a cleg and hangs on the side of the beasts at pasture, watching the Christian folk pass with his little red eyes.

JANET. If the Devil's as small as that, you needn't fear him. One slap, he's just blood on your hand, Captain.

ROSS. I've seen men swell and die from one bite. They always said that was the Devil's bite.

JANET. I've always said those were men that breathed foul air and drank black water and were none too careful where they dipped their cock or their tongue.

ROSS. So they got what they deserved?

JANET. It's not for me to say what men deserve. That's the Lord's work.

ROSS. You say his name.

JANET. And sing my psalms.

ROSS. I bet you've a bonny singing voice.

JANET. Oh, that'd charm you for sure. I've a voice could make you weep, Captain Ross.

ROSS. I'd sooner you made me smile.

JANET. Tell me how to do that and we'll maybe try it.

ROSS. I'll tell you nothing.

JANET. You can't help what I learn just from the look of you.

ROSS. And what's that?

JANET. Give me time, it'll be everything short of the smell of your soul.

ROSS. Keep your hands off my soul, woman.

JANET. I couldn't catch it and I wouldn't try. Everything else, though...

ROSS. What?

JANET. I could maybe catch that... if you let me.

ROSS. If I let you.

JANET. How else?

A beat.

ROSS. You've been a widow fifteen years.

JANET. Sixteen in November.

ROSS. That's a cold bed.

JANET. I bear it well enough.

ROSS. And warm it well enough?

A beat.

JANET. My neighbours will tell you the truth of that. You can't scratch your nose in your sleep but you wake their dogs.

ROSS. They say you're often from your bed.

JANET. How would they know unless they were from theirs?

ROSS. Well… that's not the business of my office… unless complaint is made.

JANET. I'd like to see them dare!

ROSS. They'd be afraid to risk that, would they?

JANET. Who's been calling me a whore!? Who!? Who spits that lie at me!?

ROSS. Mistress Horne, I'm not here to listen to gossip.

JANET. And why are you still here, Captain Ross?

ROSS. To talk to you.

Can we not talk a little more?

JANET. I doubt I'm too busy for conversation.

ROSS. If you've read me, as you've said you have, then you'll know I have a terrible need to talk to you.

JANET *hesitates.*

Is that how it works? You can read my face like the page of a Bible?

JANET. As clear.

If I read your hand I'd know all of you.

ROSS. Now there's an Italian trick.

JANET. But I know you'll not dare my touch, though, so…

He offers his hand, cutting her off.

ROSS. Read me.

She hesitates then takes his hand.

She reads it a moment.

Well?

JANET (*absorbed*). Well, what?

ROSS. Tell me what you see.

JANET. I'm reading the story of your life. Do you not know the story of your own life?

ROSS. Yes.

JANET. Well then.

ROSS. What of the future?

JANET *sees something. She draws in her breath sharply and drops his hand.*

What is it, witch? What's in my future?

JANET. Less than you want.

More than you deserve.

She looks at him, studying him, frightened, excited.

ROSS. What is it?

JANET. Oh, I'll not fear you. I'll not. I'll show you how little I fear you.

She touches him.

Do your worst.

NIALL *enters with* ELSPETH *and* DOUGLAS. HELEN *trails behind.*

ROSS *gets up, turning to greet them, calm, quietly in control.*

ROSS. Douglas Begg, Mistress Begg. We're glad to see you.

(*Taking* DOUGLAS*'s hand.*) I've not met you since I came, Mr Begg. It's your land down the hill there?

DOUGLAS. Aye, sir.

ROSS. That's bonny pasture. Well-drained.

DOUGLAS. It is, sir, and thank you.

ROSS. And you're the town locksmith as well?

DOUGLAS. I am, sir.

ROSS. Well, that makes you town jailer and executioner too, doesn't it? If we've need of you?

DOUGLAS (*taken aback*). Eh... It does but...

ROSS. Oh, don't worry. I've found some tinks with chicken feathers round their mouths this afternoon but we'll send for troops from Inverness to take them for hanging. It'll not be your work.

DOUGLAS. I don't fear work, sir, but...

ROSS (*cutting him off*). Is this the woman?

JANET. Douglas Begg, what have you been saying about me?

DOUGLAS. The truth. You're a witch.

JANET. Call me what names you like, Douglas. I'm just your neighbour, Janet Horne, for all your name-calling.

ROSS. You deny cursing this man's beasts?

JANET. There's power in me a beetle like him should fear. I'll not deny that.

ROSS. Then you confess your wickedness.

JANET. There's none in me that the Bible wouldn't allow. An eye for an eye, mebbe... If you've a stick in your hand and a dog means to bite you, you'll strike him.

ROSS. What do you say, minister? Is it a crime before God to practise sorcery?

JANET. Oh, don't go asking him anything. If a rat ate his shoelaces he'd be too scared to kick it.

NIALL. I'm here to speak for you, Janet.

JANET. Oh, choke on it, you big clump of docks. Flapping about, trying to take the sting out of everything. I've a sharp enough tongue in my own head.

ROSS. Your anger's up.

JANET. I'll not stand accused on my own doorstep.

HELEN. Mother...

JANET. And you be quiet as well.

ROSS. Is this your daughter. May I see her hands?

JANET. You keep your fingers off my chick!

ROSS (*to* HELEN). Show me your hands, Helen.

JANET. I'm warning you, master...!

ROSS. What will you do? Will you curse me?

JANET. If I did, you'd know its weight when it fell on you.

ROSS *helps himself to* HELEN's *hands, examining them.* JANET *darts forward.*

ROSS (*calm*). If you strike an officer of the law you'll hang for sure.

ELSPETH *puts a hand on* JANET, *holding her back.*

(*To* HELEN.) Your feet the same?

HELEN. Yes.

ROSS. Well... it's not so bad. As if you'd burnt them in a fire.

(*He turns on* JANET.) Maybe that's a sign you got her with the Devil...

JANET. I got her with Angus Horne, more fool me...

ROSS (*cutting her off*). I understand the Devil's mark is a subtler thing, a little nip somewhere on your skin. We'd have to strip the clothes off you and search it out with a pin.

JANET. Oh, you'd like to try that? In front of them all?

ROSS. But I'm inclined to believe you're a poorer creature than that.

JANET. Poor?

ROSS. Just a widow tricking scraps of food out of her ignorant neighbours. I don't see so much harm in you. Just mean, grasping malice.

JANET. Is that right?

DOUGLAS. Did he just call us ignorant?

ROSS. You're no witch. I know their look and there's none of that black power in you.

JANET. Oh, you know the look of a witch?

DOUGLAS. He did, eh? He's calling us ignorant?

ROSS *(ignoring this)*. A dishonest beggar. Is that what we'll call you? Anyway. If there's more complaint I'll see you whipped, but the law doesn't need to worry itself with the likes of you.

A beat.

JANET. Oh, and you so bonny with the silver buttons on your coat. However did you end up in Dornoch, Captain Ross?

Have you some aunty knows the Laird of Loth and got you some wee job no other body wanted?

How did you come to that? A fine boy like you with a sword on his hip?

ROSS *(to* NIALL*)*. You're right. There's nothing here. We'll leave this poor creature to her mumbling.

JANET *(stopping him)*. Oh, here now! Where are you off to? Were you not after hearing your life story?

ROSS. Not from your mouth.

JANET. But it's a great story, isn't it? Our Captain Ross is a military man after all. He's seen men break like waves on the battlefield. Is that not what you told me? Is that where you saw the witches as well?

She reads his slight reaction.

It was, eh? On the battlefield! And you just a beardless wee boy. What age were you when the swords were last rattling, Captain Ross, fourteen, fifteen years old?

ROSS. Old enough to serve.

JANET. Oh God, that must have been a terror. No strength in your wee arms to hold your sword straight. Men screaming and smashing limbs all around you...

Is there a mark on you? Did they cut you down?

ROSS *says nothing.*

No! Because you saw the hags on the battlefield. So you must have been lying with the dead.

Is that what you did? Did you hear the roar of hooves and feet and clashing blades bearing down on you and flop down in your own terror piss, lying still... still like the corpses that crashed about you, still, still... till the last hacking blow had stopped shaking the crying men that lay around you... and the dark came... and the thirst was greater than your terror... So you opened your eyes... and saw them. Dark, ragged-haired hags, cutting the silver rings off the dead...? Did she touch you? Did she put a hand on your warm skin, wanting it cold enough to plunder? Did you leap away and run off crying into the dark?

Did you hear her come flying after you? Did you look behind you and see her great, death-stinking, flapping-cloth wings... reaching after you?

She's reading that she's hitting the mark, from his face.

Aye, I read it in your hand, Captain.

You're the one that knows witches. You're the one that's seen the Devil.

He came down the hill for you... hacking men up when they were still living, didn't he? Just a man to look at, but that red beast's in him when the blade's in his hand. Don't be frightened, wee Captain. You're just a boy. How could you stand against the Devil? He knows tricks you'll always be too scared to learn. No, they've sent you to Dornoch so you can sleep your wee life away as gentle as a fieldmouse curled up under winter leaves. No shame in it, Davey Ross. No one here cares that you'd not the courage to lift your sword. Was your mammy awful disappointed in her smiling boy? You're just a wee boy after all. How can you command the power that sends men storming down a hill to break like water on the rocks? It's not in you, is it? You'd fall over if a witch woman blew on you.

Suddenly, JANET jumps at him, blowing and clapping.

Involuntarily, ROSS steps backwards. He falls over, ELSPETH's bucket falls over him.

He struggles to get up. DOUGLAS struggles not to laugh.

ROSS (*the contents of the bucket stink*). Jesus, what...?

ELSPETH. Oh, sir! I'm so sorry.

She goes to help him.

JANET. Mind! He'll get it on your skirts, Elspeth!

ROSS. What...?

DOUGLAS (*hearty*). Ah, it's clean muck, sir, never you worry.

ELSPETH. It's from the pigs, sir... a present for Janet's wee vegetable garden.

ELSPETH *and* NIALL *are helping* ROSS *up.*

DOUGLAS. It's just the stink of it, sir. It'll not harm the cloth.

ROSS *gives* JANET *one angry look.*

JANET. Nothing else to say, Captain Ross?

Well, if you find a use for your anger, you know where I live.

ROSS *exits.*

NIALL (*following*). You'll not let yourself be helped, Janet, will you?

JANET. Oh, and how could you help me? One foot on either bank of the stream, feart of falling your whole days. Away and find an opinion, minister.

NIALL *exits,* DOUGLAS *following, still chuckling.*

DOUGLAS. You're an evil stoat of a woman, Janet, but you're an entertainment. I'll give you that.

DOUGLAS *exits.* ELSPETH *is laughing.* HELEN *is terrified.*

HELEN. He'll come for you.

JANET. Oh, Helen! The face on you!

HELEN. He'll come for you. He will.

JANET. Let him try. I'll turn myself to a fat hen and shit on his shoes, I'll turn myself to a dancing frog and leap out his hands, I'll turn myself to smoke and blind and choke him… let him try and put his irons on me then!

HELEN. But you can't do that! You can't! You know you can't. Tell him it's all lies. Please.

A beat.

JANET. Stop your crying.

HELEN. You can't.

Tell him you can't.

JANET. You don't know what I can do.

HELEN. You can't even…

You can't even…

JANET. I can't what!?

No! Tell me! What is it you're daring me to?

HELEN. If you called the Devil out of the trees… would he come…?

JANET. Yes.

And if you laid your eyes on the Devil, a silly little girl like you, do you think there's one bit of you that wouldn't be eaten up?

HELEN (*whisper*). No.

JANET. No.

So you'll not be seeing him tonight.

You don't know what you're talking about. Stupid girl. Leave my work to me like I've told you to and stop your fuss.

HELEN. He's angry. He'll hurt you.

JANET. How can he catch me?

How can he catch me now?

They're just looking at her. HELEN *desperate.* ELSPETH *with growing uncertainty.*

(*Changing her tone.*) There now… there… are you worrying over nothing? Are you a bairn again, crying over air and fancies? Shall I give you sugar and sing you back to sleep?

HELEN. We've no sugar now. We've nothing.

JANET. You just see what I can make with nothing. Sit you down now. Sit you down on the bank.

They obey. JANET *lifts her jug and passes it to them.*

There now. Take a drink while I see what I can get you.

ELSPETH (*drinks*). Oh, that's cool in my throat. What's in that?

JANET. Just water from the burn.

ELSPETH. There's something… (*Tasting it in her mouth.*) Something… tastes green.

JANET. Now.

Tell me, Elspeth. What have you a fancy to eat?

ELSPETH. No, no, Janet, I know you've nothing in, just…

JANET. Take another wee drink, Elspeth… What does that give you a hunger for… warm bread?

ELSPETH. Oh, I'll take a piece of that any day, but...

JANET. White bread?

ELSPETH. Oh! As if I'd ever get another taste of that! Maybe at my table in heaven...

JANET. Brown crust broken open, steam rising out the white dough inside...

ELSPETH (*seeing it*). Oh!

JANET. Smell the warm-yeast breath of it? What'll we put on that? A wee bit cream, maybe...

ELSPETH. Oh, we can't eat the cream...

JANET. There's plenty left for market. Just put a dab on that hot bread, Elspeth... Aw, it's melting in, isn't it, making the warm crust soft... What else? A wee bit salt? Fresh onion?

ELSPETH. Honey! Honey!

JANET. I'll break a comb over it, let the golden sweet flow all over...

ELSPETH (*tasting it*). Oh!

JANET. Watch you don't get your fingers sticky, Elspeth, take another wee drink to wash it down.

ELSPETH *grabs the jug off* HELEN, *who's drinking deeply.*

HELEN. Meat.

JANET. You want meat, pet?

HELEN. And gravy.

JANET. Oh, when was the last time we had meat? Beef, was it? Venison?

HELEN. I don't care! I don't care! Just...

JANET. Oh, a good, fat joint of pork then. Taste that, Helen, salt on the crackling, brown and crunching from the flame... Aw, bite into that, my sweetheart, feel the hot fat on your chin.

HELEN. And fruit... and soft apples... and brambles and...

JANET. Never mind your soft apples. Here, I'll give you something you've never had. I'll give you an orange.

ELSPETH. What...?

HELEN. Where...?

JANET. Shhh! Look, look, see, it's in my hand. Like a wee sun, see how the light glows in it? See how pretty? I can pick these off the trees like berries off a haw. So many little suns in the dark-green leaves.

Now I'll open it... see... split it with my nails... Can you smell the perfume of that? That's the sun in its skin, sharp and sweet in your nose... and look inside... a piece for each of us... inside the wee sun are little orange moons... Take one... there... now bite it... Taste that... sharper than a rasp... sweeter than an apple... a taste that makes your whole mouth clean and full of light... You're eating the sun and the moon together...

HELEN. I can taste it!

ELSPETH. Aw, that's lovely...

JANET. You feast on that while I get us some music. What do you think? Shall we have a fiddler?

ELSPETH. I love a good fiddler.

JANET. I know, Elspeth. I've heard the stories. Shall we have a reel out of him? Can you hear him?

ELSPETH. Naw... I can't just...

JANET. Aye, you can! He's just walking up from the shore... hear him? He's playing 'Thomas the Rhymer'...

ELSPETH. Oh, I love that one.

JANET. He's closer now, oh, that man's working his bow like he's slicing the air... Hear the silver sound of him?

ELSPETH. I hear it now!

Oh, I can dance to that.

Oh! Oh, can you see her, Janet?! There! Her skirts twirling.

JANET. She's a bonny dancer.

ELSPETH. Oh, my darling wee thing. I'll dance with you again. Never mind your daddy frowning at us.

ELSPETH's on her feet. Starting to dance. HELEN *is taking a drink,* JANET *is close beside her.*

JANET. Are you dancing, Helen?

HELEN (*enraptured*). Yes!

She hands the jug to her mother and starts to dance. JANET *half-dances alongside her, speaking quiet and close, just to her.*

JANET. See, I know you and I know what you are...

You've a fancy to dance off and leave me, Helen, haven't you? Aren't you full-grown these five years? Younger girls than you feeding big, kicking bairns...

HELEN. I could have a bairn.

JANET. Of course you could. Of course. But I'll not be the widow alone on the hill, Helen. And I'll not have some fat farting fool of a Mackenzie lording it in my house and calling my earth his.

If you could be a bird. If you could fly like a gull to France. If you could dance on a wave. I'd let you go for ever. I'd even let you go just a spit down the hill to waste yourself in kissing a man that smells of seed and cow shit. But you can't do anything, Helen, you're just the rock that holds my foot in the earth...

HELEN. I can fly...

JANET. Aye, you can fly with my voice in your ear... but if I stop singing, you drop down in the dirt like a wee marionette with your strings cut... Your feet as heavy as wood, your grubby wee fingers staining my skirts as you grab for me... Well, if that's how it is, Helen, if I'm your prisoner yet, you'll dance to my tune, milady, hear me?

HELEN. I'll dance.

JANET. Aye, you'll dance where I set you. You can dance yourself up the sky. You can sit on the moon and laugh at the
earth far beneath you like a leaping hare, Helen... but only if
I let you... only with my music in you. You've none of your
own, for all I've taught you.

You're made of the Dornoch mud I dropped you out onto
and I'm cursed to love you in all your twisted disappointment.

Dance then! Dance like you could charm your legs yourself!

ELSPETH *has worn herself out, slumped dozing on the
ground. It's getting dark.* HELEN *dances faster and faster.*

ELSPETH. Oh, I can see her. I can see her. My bonny girl.
Dancing holes in her shoes. She was always on the shore,
dancing with the sea. The white sails... The white sails
fooled her... They look like great ladies waltzing home in
wedding dresses... What did she know of the men that raise
those sails...? A sailor's bairn in her and she died in her
father's heart the minute she told us... But she's not dead...
she's not... Out lost... Dancing on cold roads without shoes
and feart ever to come home again...

Scene Five

HELEN *is up in the sky. She's a horse, galloping faster and
faster up into the stars. She's struggling, trying to throw an
invisible rider.*

HELEN. Get off my back! Get off my back!

*She's galloped right up to the moon. It's a huge harvest moon
looming over her.*

NICK *walks out of the moon. He has a bunch of hawthorn in
his hand and a lantern.*

NICK. Where are you riding to, lassie?

HELEN (*struggling*). Get her off my back!

NICK. You're here alone.

HELEN (*bent*). I can feel her, feel her heels in my sides...! Aw! Rot her! I'll ride her off me!

NICK. You'll not get far like that, lassie. You're a twisted creature now.

HELEN. I'm not!

NICK. Look at you! Bent over like a begging crone.

HELEN. I'm not!

NICK. Twisted wee thing, begging me to shift nothing at all off her own back...

HELEN *shoots upright and flies at him.*

HELEN. I'll ride you down as well, you Devil!

HELEN *stops. A young woman again.*

NICK. So you've bonny straight legs after all.

She's standing on the hillside under a huge moon. She feels her back.

HELEN (*wonder*). She wasn't there.

NICK. No one here but you, the moon and the Devil.

A beat.

HELEN. What are you doing here?

NICK *points down the hill.*

NICK. See the fires? The cockle-pickers, the travelling folk are sitting up at the top of the shore, watching the night. I'm on my way to sit with them a while.

HELEN. Are you a travelling man?

NICK. Of course.

HELEN. Have you been to Italy?

NICK. No. Nor yet to England. My feet turn at the border. This is my road.

HELEN. Why are you stopping?

NICK. That… I'm not sure of.

HELEN. Why are you looking at me so?

He says nothing.

Do you want to lie with me?

NICK. I would. Are you asking me?

HELEN. No.

NICK. Well then.

HELEN. Won't you just please yourself anyway?

NICK. No. The Devil can't go where he's not invited.

A beat.

HELEN. I don't think you're old enough to be the Devil. I don't think you're so much older than me.

NICK. Maybe so. But that's old enough.

A beat.

HELEN. I'm not asking you for anything. Why are you still here?

NICK. Well… I suppose I'd a fancy to chase you. But you don't seem to be running away. It's alarming.

HELEN. Why would I run away?

NICK. It's customary.

HELEN. Maybe you're the one that should run.

NICK. Maybe.

I can't sit with them. The travellers. I sit at the edge of the fire and watch them. They won't look at me. They're afraid.

HELEN. You can't hold hawthorn.

NICK. Why not?

HELEN. That's a holy flower. That keeps you away.

NICK. I like the smell of it. And the bonny white flowers.

(*Offers it to her*.) Here, you hold it then.

HELEN *steps back*.

HELEN. I want nothing from you.

NICK. It was freely offered. Freely meant.

He puts it on the ground between them. Waits.

HELEN *doesn't move*.

I used to walk the roads of men and now I walk the roads just beside them. How did that happen?

HELEN *says nothing*.

Maybe I was a boy playing with stones on the shore. Maybe they drove me away... with pebbles hot from the sun, wet from the sea.

They drove me away. They drove me out into the dark, on my own. They're afraid of what they see in me. So I'm alone. But now you're here.

How did you come here?

HELEN *says nothing*.

I need to be on my road. Will you be following me?

HELEN (*scorn*). No!

Why? Are you asking me to?

NICK. I don't ask for anything either.

But you said you would have no master but me.

A beat.

HELEN (*whisper*). I lied.

NICK (*laughs*). Well... it won't kill you.

He holds something out to her. It's her little silver knife.

This for your lie and there's no debts between us.

(*He pockets the knife again.*) You're company. For as long as you stand there. I'm hungry for that. Something like me.

HELEN. I am nothing like you!

NICK. Then how can you see me? How can you talk with me?

They'll drive you out soon. You'll walk the same road as me whether you will or not.

HELEN (*whisper*). They should kill me first.

NICK (*laughs*). Oh, they'll try.

You're not so young at all and they'll know it. It's not your hands, lassie. It was never your bonny hands and feet, don't comfort yourself with that. It's what's in your eyes that'll terrify the love out of them. I tried hiding in a wee boy's body, a smiling loon, a loving son... They saw me in the end.

HELEN. I am nothing like you.

NICK. They pushed me in the fire but I walked out whole. Then we all knew.

HELEN. Stop your talking...

NICK. There's no rider on your back. And you've held the Devil on the road when he was wanting to be walking.

A beat.

HELEN (*quiet*). And could she do that?

NICK. Who?

HELEN. My mother.

A beat.

NICK. We've never spoken. I don't know the woman.

A beat.

HELEN. I can feel your breath.

NICK. And?

HELEN. It's soft and hot.

NICK. Sometimes it is.

This is how it will be. You'll see something, a rabbit, a hare, a hoody crow… You'll think to take its life like snatching up a tinker's ribbons… and in a blink it'll be dead before you. Because you can make life or take life like braiding ribbons in your hair.

HELEN. God spare me your ill-wishing.

NICK. I'd like to see him try.

NICK *walks away into the dark.*

After a moment, HELEN *picks up the hawthorn. She smells it.*

She exits in the opposite direction to NICK.

Scene Six

Near Janet Horne's house – later that same night.

JANET *stands in the warm dark.*

JANET. I think I might never grow old. There's not a line on my face.

I'm rooted in this cold earth and yet the tree's full of sap. What do you think? Am I green and supple yet?

Plenty women are withered to dust at my age. Dead in damp graves. But I'm as full of juice as an autumn bramble. Maybe age has tried creeping up on me and I've just heard the rustle of her dead, dry feet in the bracken and turned and flashed my eyes at her… Oh yes… look at the old fool run, hunchback, stumbling, pissing herself in dottled terror… Never. That'll never be me. Never. Maybe I'll live for ever.

Maybe I'll see the nights and days flow past me like the shadows of clouds on the hills and I'll be warm and wet and growing yet... year after year...

A man comes to stand behind her. We don't see him clearly at first. It's ROSS.

What do you think?

ROSS *embraces her. She laughs, holding him to her.*

I knew where your anger would take you. Didn't I? See the charm I work, Captain Ross? See what I can do?

Who has the power, Davey boy? You or me?

He's lost in her, she pushes him away.

Tell me. I want to hear you say it. Who has the power now? Who brought you here? Who kept you here? Who knows your soul better than you ever will?

He stares at her, saying nothing.

If you won't speak it's because you know truth when you hear it. Speak to me, Davey. Tell me you're the one with the power after all.

He still says nothing.

(*Laughs.*) Then I own you now, boy. Did you think to rule this wee town? Lording it over these fields of salty grass? Well, I'm the law here, Davey. Know it. Swallow it. Surrender and keep your mouth shut about me and mine.

He still says nothing. She pats his face.

Good boy. On your way then. I'm needing my bed.

JANET *exits.*

ROSS *just stands, getting himself together. He's full of tight emotion.*

HELEN *comes on, staggering, dragging the hawthorn. She's almost sleepwalking.*

She stops when she sees ROSS, *swaying.*

ROSS. Helen.

HELEN. Who are you?

ROSS. It's the sheriff. Captain Ross.

Where have you been?

HELEN. Up into the sky.

He's sensing the state she's in; he's quiet, predatory.

ROSS. How did you get up there, sweetheart?

HELEN. Mother... Mother...

ROSS. Yes?

HELEN. She made me her horse... her dappled pony... See my hands... see...? She's nailed silver horseshoes to my hands and feet, and rides me into the sky...

ROSS. Does it hurt?

HELEN. Oh yes, sir... yes... she hurts me sore... but I shook her off my back tonight... I shook her off!

ROSS. Well done.

HELEN. She'll not be master of me... I threw her off as I galloped past the moon... She was riding me up into the dark beyond the moon... and the Devil...

ROSS. Yes?

HELEN. The Devil came out of the moon to meet me...

ROSS. You talked with the Devil?

HELEN. Yes...

ROSS. And your mother sent you there?

HELEN. She knows where that road starts but I rode it... I did... Oh, sir, I am so tired...

ROSS. Lie down... lie down on the bank here... I'll cover you with my coat...

She lets him guide her down. He puts his coat over her.

HELEN. She'll not use me so... My poor hands and feet...

ROSS. Shhhh... sleep now.

HELEN (*nearly unconscious*). She'll not be on my back again.

ROSS. No. It's over now. It's over.

HELEN. It's no magic. It's just herbs she puts in the water, see. She thinks I don't know. But I do.

I know where the power is now, God help me, sir. I know. They should kill me. I'll never hurt any of God's creatures. He can't make me.

(*Half-sleeping, half-crying.*) Don't let them kill me, sir. Don't let them burn me.

ROSS (*soothing*). Shhh... No one will hurt you.

HELEN. They should burn it out of me. They should.

HELEN *is asleep.* ROSS *sits watching over her, looking up at the moon.*

End of Act One.

ACT TWO

Scene One

A cell in the church tower.

JANET *has been chained to the wall. She is wearing just bits of sack, cold and filthy. She has not been allowed to sleep for days.*

It is now frosty autumn.

She is old and frightened and exhausted. DOUGLAS *is holding part of the chain that tethers her.*

He is nearly asleep. Nodding where he sits.

JANET *is seeing him doze. She's talking to him quietly, a soothing lullaby.*

JANET. It's cold now, Douglas… There's a crackle of frost on the ground… no wind… the trees stand bare and still without their leaves… they're sleeping… no air stirs them… freezing fog like a blanket wrapped through the silent branches… and down below… deep in the stone-hard earth… the beetles and quick wriggling worms are all still and sleeping, curled up small… pebbles of life… barely moving… waiting in the dark… the hedgehog's safe in his ball of leaves… prickles turned out to war with the icicles, closed in over his own core of warmth, like a wee coal he's breathing on in the night… keeping warm… keeping warm… sleeping…

As DOUGLAS *drops further into his doze,* JANET *is edging down onto the floor, still talking him to sleep, nearly dropping herself.*

The thrush is dozing in his nest. All the snails are frozen in their shells. All the berries ice on the twig. Too hard for him to eat. He's keeping a hungry belly warm with downy feathers and dry wisps of wool, crouched in his nest's lining… cuddling into his own heart's heat… safe in the nest, Douglas… safe till spring… sleeping… sleeping… sleeping…

DOUGLAS *is snoring softly,* JANET *eases herself down, sleeping as soon as her body touches the floor.*

As she slumps, the chain tightens between them, jerking DOUGLAS *awake. He yanks on it, pulling* JANET *up, roaring with rage and frustration.*

DOUGLAS. Wake up, you bitch! Wake up!

JANET *is crying with exhaustion and despair.*

JANET. Oh God, let me sleep! Please, Douglas! Please! If you're Christian at all, let me sleep!

DOUGLAS. You'll not sleep. Not till you've talked the Devil out of you. Not till you've told us all the sin that's in you. Tell us what you are, bitch!

JANET. You know what I am, Douglas! You know all that I am, you've seen me every day these twenty years!

DOUGLAS. Aye, and I know you for a black-hearted witch!

JANET. I've never harmed you or yours!

DOUGLAS. Two beasts dead! A quarter of all my wealth, food for flies! We couldn't even eat the flesh, it swelled in the pot to a grey mess that stank of your foul cursing…

JANET. I never cursed your beasts, Douglas, I never did…!

DOUGLAS. And didn't you boast of it, in front of us all? Dancing your wickedness in my face and gloating like a cat with a wee bird dying in its claws…

JANET. I didn't do it!

DOUGLAS. You know you did! Just like you know what you are and you will confess it! You will! If I have to stay chained to your grimy bones another hundred years, you'll speak the truth at last, bitch!

JANET. Oh, Douglas… please…!

DOUGLAS. Because you know what else you did! You brought the Devil down to rule us all. Who knew there was so much law in the whole world? Things written down that stop a man driving his beasts where he will or drawing water where he's found it twenty, thirty years... Laws to stop you eating what you find in the hedges in case it's some other man's fruit... I know my letters and I couldn't read so much law before I slept in my grave!

JANET. We can sleep a bit before that, though, Douglas. We can.

DOUGLAS. He's brought a score of troops down, from Inverness, up and down, up and down, they've stamped from one end of the parish to the other and not a house has been spared. They've had their cudgels out and taken coin from every Christian soul that's breathing here.

He'd've had us all in irons if he wasn't needing them all to tie you down quiet.

You're a meddling witch, Janet Horne. You saw the mad dog sleeping in the sun and did you not have to stick out your naughty foot and stir the beast! Rot you! Tell me what you are and let me go free!

JANET. I'm just Janet from up the hill, Douglas...

DOUGLAS (*cutting over her*). What did I do... What did I do to have you a stone tied to my legs... drowning me... you bitch?... Why am I sat here in this cold cell waiting on you... needing my bed... night after night after night... It's not me should be here...

JANET. No. No, you can leave me a while... you can rest...

DOUGLAS. It's not my job to stay here... hour after hour... a morning, maybe... a night or two...

JANET. It's not fair... they shouldn't make you do it...

DOUGLAS. They should not... Where's the sheriff? Where's the minister? If the Devil comes out of you, what am I to do?

JANET. They shouldn't leave you to do it all, Douglas... it's not fair on you...

DOUGLAS. I've animals to feed! I've folk waiting on locks that'd pay me money that could feed us all! But no...

JANET. No...

DOUGLAS. I'm stuck...

JANET. Stuck here with me.

DOUGLAS. It's not right.

JANET. It's a black shame. And you needing your bed as bad as me...

DOUGLAS. God, to put my head down for five minutes...

JANET. You deserve that, Douglas... You've worked so hard...

DOUGLAS. The minister and the sheriff lying under sheets every night...

JANET. Feather pillows under their heads...

DOUGLAS. The Devil send them black dreams.

JANET. Rot them.

DOUGLAS. This is not my work...

JANET. It's not.

DOUGLAS. I should be sleeping.

JANET. We'll just close our eyes for a few moments, Douglas, just doze a little while... There's no harm in it...

DOUGLAS. Oh God, I'm so tired...

JANET. Just sleep, Douglas... sleep...

DOUGLAS. I'm not allowed... I'm not allowed until the minister comes to take his turn.

JANET. But that's not fair... that's not...

DOUGLAS (*cutting her off*). Fair or not. Someone has to break you.

A beat.

JANET (*whisper*). I'm broken already, Douglas. I'm just cold dust on the floor. Let me lie down.

DOUGLAS. Not till you've talked the Devil out of you.

NIALL enters.

In Christ's name, where have you been? You're a day late! Here!

He hands NIALL *the chain. Lies down on the floor and is instantly asleep.*

NIALL *holds the chain and stands looking at* JANET.

JANET. Let me lie down, minister.

Let me lie down.

NIALL. I walked to Tain. The minister is a good friend. An old friend...

JANET. Please...

NIALL. Janet... I have to do right by you... That's the most important thing.

JANET. So let me sleep.

NIALL. I haven't known what to do for the best.

JANET. All I want is to rest my head on the floor, even on the stone floor...

NIALL. No one has even heard of such a thing... thought of such a thing... all my working life... So. I went to the man who taught me all I am.

JANET. Just for one strike of the clock. Just till the quarter...

NIALL. His soul is good, Janet. As honest as freshwater. His heart has no doubt, every beat a certain solid knock of true faith... He's more than my father.

JANET. Did he teach you pity, minister? Did he?

NIALL. Oh, he's old now... It hurt me to see it. I had to take his arm and help him to his chair...

JANET. Dozing, in his chair, was he? Before the fire? Oh Christ...

NIALL. He could see I'd come with great trouble in my heart, so... though I'd not seen him these five years and might not see him living again, he wasted no time offering me tea or whisky to warm me from the journey...

JANET. Tea... or whisky... hot in your belly... Oh God...

NIALL. So I told him. I told him I knew an honest woman... no harm in her but a few mumbled charms and a bad temper...

JANET. Oh, bless you, minister, bless you, it's the truth, the truth...

NIALL. ...That she'd been under my care these ten years and sometimes in the church...

JANET. More than sometimes, minister... as often as my work spared me...

NIALL. And now she's in a cell in the church tower...

JANET. Chained like a dog!

NIALL. Waiting sentence for witchcraft...

JANET. It's a black lie, minister, what they say about me... you know it is...

NIALL. Well, it troubled him, Janet. He thought a long time. He went to speak and then thought better so he prayed a while and then he spoke at last...

JANET. And he spoke mercy, minister, didn't he...?

NIALL. He asked me one thing, Janet, his old eyes fixed on my face, trying to see the truth clear... though he can barely see a human face at all unless the sun is full upon it... his sight is failing but like a good loyal old sheepdog he still strains to see his flock and...

JANET (*cutting in*). Yes! Yes! What did he ask? What did he say?

NIALL. He said, 'Niall, Niall, to your certain knowledge has this woman ever attempted charms or tricks or anything that denied the power of God as the only force for good and ill in the world...?'

JANET. Well, you couldn't say I'd done that, no, just a wee bit magic, just a wee bit help to needy friends…

NIALL. And I said, 'Yes, I've seen her put her hands on beasts to cure them. I've seen her try and raise the weather. I've seen her curse.'

JANET. But that's all, it's true, and the cursing's only when I'm sore provoked.

NIALL. And he said, and there were tears in those old eyes when he said it, Janet… he said… 'Then the law of God is clear, Niall, and the law of man is clear… and the best help you can be to that poor body is to bring her to true understanding and remorse of what she's done…'

JANET. What does he mean? Remorse? Do I not look like I'm brimming over with remorse?

NIALL (*close to tears*). Oh, and Janet, I've failed you.

JANET. No, you've not. What do you mean? No, you'll help me…

NIALL (*over this*). I've failed you because you have been under my care these ten years and I let my own pride, my own dislike of that man…

JANET. Oh God, minister, he's an awful man, save me from that sheriff, save me…

NIALL (*over this*)….blind me to the truth that was in my face!

JANET. I'm so sorry I laughed at you, minister. I know I angered you. I know… but I meant no harm… I just open my mouth and toads fall out. I don't know what I'm saying…

NIALL. No. I'm not angry any more, Janet. But I see my fault in this.

I let you turn to the Devil and never put out my hand to pull you back. Well, my hand's out now. My hand's out now. Hold on and we'll get through this together.

JANET. Your hand's out? Where are you taking me?

NIALL. To forgiveness, Janet. To the peace of your confession of guilt. And though they will kill you for it... I'll stand beside you. I won't leave you alone in the dark again.

A beat.

JANET. Well, you can take your holy helping hand and shove it up to have a poke at your own shite!

For the love of Christ! What's wrong with you!? Can you hear yourself?! Bumbling on like a fat bee caught in a cobweb!

The evil piece of dog vomit's going to kill me! He's going to burn me alive! And you stand there gumming away at psalms and weeping like the hot tar's going to be scalding your soft skin! No! It's me he's killing, minister! Save my life or go drown yourself in your own privy! And I hope you die with your mouth open!

ROSS *enters on the end of this speech. He laughs.*

ROSS. Is that her confession, minister?

NIALL. No. No, it's not. She's not broken yet.

ROSS. Well... Well, what are we to do?

You know what you've to do, minister?

NIALL. Yes.

ROSS. Then go to it.

NIALL *exits.* ROSS *takes the chain and sits watching* JANET*, tugging gently if she ever seems to be fading out.*

How long have we kept you here, Janet?

JANET. Two months.

ROSS. And how long have we kept you awake?

JANET. I don't know... I've no days now... only this chain and Douglas Begg's fat hand on it...

ROSS. We've kept you awake for four days and five nights. Do you know why we've done it?

JANET. To hurt me.

ROSS. To let you see the Devil in you. Have you seen him yet?

JANET. I saw the stones in the walls moving as if they were breathing. I saw worms crawling out of my skin. I saw a spider on the floor with my mother's face and she asked me why I was crying.

ROSS. You're dreaming with your eyes open. That's good. You'll see him soon.

JANET. What are you waiting for? Why don't you kill me?

ROSS. I'm an officer of the law, Janet. It wouldn't be legal. Confess you renounced your baptism. Confess you took the Devil as your master and then we'll make an end.

JANET. I say my prayers like everyone else. I'm praying to God to save me from the sight of you.

ROSS. Then you've no power, is that what you're saying?

JANET. You know the power I have…

ROSS. There's no shame in it.

It'll spare your life, Janet. Just tell me how you lied.

JANET. About what?

ROSS. You couldn't charm the skin off a pan of milk… could you?

JANET. You know me.

ROSS. You're a sad old woman with dirt under her fingernails from gripping on to a few withered sods of land. And the only way you can feed yourself and your twisted get is to whine and dance and terrify your neighbours into giving you crusts to stop your curses.

JANET. You'll know the power of my cursing soon. You wait…

ROSS. You couldn't scare a fly off your face if it saw you as I do.

JANET. You'll see my rage and tremble, boy… You'll know my hating when it's choking you…

ROSS. A limping, mumbling, stinking old hag that's too proud to beg but you're a beggar even so… isn't that right?

A liar.

A cheat. A thief without the decency to pick pockets. You have to fumble your fingers over people's thoughts and souls. Dazzling honest hearts with your cheap tricks. A sham.

JANET. No.

ROSS. Yes.

You know it.

Now, say it's so and you can sleep before we put you out in the churchyard as a common thief. You can doze as the honest folk of Dornoch spit at you and point you out to their children as a liar and a thief. Mad Janet Horne who was so dottled she fancied herself a witch. They'll mock you to the end of your days, but you can have those days, Janet. I'll let you have that mouldy heel of life. You have no power, Janet. It's me that has the power over you. Isn't that so? Janet?

She says nothing.

Tell me the truth now and you can live.

JANET. What do you see? When you look at me?

ROSS. I see you clear now.

JANET *pulls herself up. She moves close to him. She almost touches him.*

JANET. Then give us another kiss, Davey, for old time's sake.

He pushes her away, revulsion.

ROSS. Get off me, you stinking whore!

JANET. Oh, you see me clear, do you, Captain Ross? You see me clear now? What do you see?

A dribbling skull? Withered dugs and reeking holes? Aye, you run from me, you'll not look on terror like this, will you? This is what the wombs that bear men come to, sucking dark and bony hips, death swallowing you whole even as it's pushing against you and grabbing your arse and crying your name. That's what you see now, eh?

ROSS. Even your breath reeks.

JANET. It does. I've every kind of foul mouth and ever kind of filth upon me and so tell me, Captain Ross... why would a man like you lie with the likes of me?

Why would a young, golden, bonny lad like you put his face between these dropping tits and put his mouth all over this withered skin and push his way into my dry cavern and groan and moan and sweat his shining silver lust upon me and when he's done roll me over and beg me to let him do it again? How could that happen, Davey Ross? Do you think?

Did you think me beautiful then?

He says nothing.

No?

Well then, do you think maybe I charmed you, Davey? Do you think you were a wee bit bewitched?   *girl stop*

He says nothing.

It's one or the other, eh? Either I've the power to make you leap in my bed, or you wanted this hag, Davey. Wanted me so bad you pushed me over when I tried to bar the door against you.

You were hard before I even touched you.

Who did you want, Davey? The witch or the woman? Is it you that's a fancy to put his mouth where the Devil's been? Confess the truth, Davey, then we'll maybe both walk free.

ROSS. You're foul.

JANET. Then you better fear me, laddie, because you've danced my tune once already.

A beat.

ROSS. I'll keep you waking till you say what the law needs to hear before it can burn you.

JANET. You'll close your eyes before I do, Davey. As I remember it, you couldn't stay awake long enough to satisfy me last time either. LOL !

A beat.

ROSS. All right then.

ROSS *exits*. JANET *sways, she half-collapses. Before she can pass out,* ROSS *is back. He's followed by* NIALL, *leading* HELEN.

HELEN *is carrying a bundle.*

JANET. Oh God, no! Not my baby!

HELEN. Mother…

JANET. Oh, my wee girl! What have they done to you?!

NIALL. She's not been harmed, Janet.

ROSS. Not kept waking, not starved or frozen or whipped…

JANET. Oh, Helen, how are you managing? Who's feeding you?

HELEN. Elspeth…

JANET. Oh, God save her. Oh, I've one friend in this world. Are you eating all right? Is she giving you cheese?

HELEN. I'm helping make it.

JANET. Are you, darling? Oh, that's clever of you. My clever girl.

ROSS. Helen has come to set you free, Janet.

JANET. How? How's that? What are you talking about?

NIALL. Listen to her, Janet. You have to speak truth now, for her sake.

JANET (*dazed*). What is it?

ROSS. Helen?

A beat.

HELEN (*quiet, almost trancelike*). My mother is no witch.

JANET. Oh, that's all right, my darling... never mind what names they call me.

HELEN. She has no power. No charms. It's all words and mumbles and bits of tricks she half-remembers.

She can't even light a damp fire. And I can do that with just these hands.

She can't even put oats in our bowls. And I can do that with just one hoe and the strength of my back.

JANET (*soft*). You can, pet. You're a good, good girl.

HELEN. Once she said she'd made herself into a hare and spent all night running through the fields. She showed me her feet wet with dew and said she must sleep all day for she'd been running all night...

JANET. Oh... that was...

HELEN. But I smelt whisky on her breath and Archibald Ross brought us peats for a month after...

JANET. They don't need to hear...

HELEN. Once she said she'd called the wind to blow me into the sea, she was that angry with me... And the wind rose... but when I hid from the storm I saw her out looking for me, crying for her little bird, swearing she never could have done such a thing... It was only the east wind off the sea and I musn't hide from her...

JANET. I would never hurt you, little bird...

HELEN. She has never spoken to the Devil. Never. He doesn't even know her name.

NIALL *looks at* ROSS, *uncertain now.*

ROSS (*gentle*). And how do you know that, Helen?

HELEN. He told me so, when I met him on the road.

JANET. What are you saying, darling?

HELEN. He doesn't know her name. He's never seen her, in any of the dark places he walks. She can't call him out of the trees. She can't charm the wind. She can't heal a pig or kill a stirk. She's no witch at all.

The witch is me.

JANET. No. No!

NIALL *is shocked, he'd no idea this was coming.*

NIALL. What are you saying, Helen!?

HELEN. The witch is me.

JANET. Helen!

ROSS. Why would you say that, Helen?

HELEN. I called the Deil out of the wood… and he came. I rode up to the moon and he walked out the moon and talked to me. And he told me he never knew my mother at all. And he told me that my mother never rode on my back at all. And he told me that of the two of us, the only one that could call the Devil… was me. And I slept that night… and when I woke you'd taken my mother from me… And all this time… all this time I've let her lie here… (*Starting to break down.*)

JANET. Oh, darling, I'm fine, I'm strong, don't…

HELEN (*over this*)….I've let her lie in chains when I knew the truth…

My mother can't make a charm… but I can…

JANET. And who sent you to the moon, Helen? Who sent you?

HELEN. She makes you swallow sweet herbs so you think you see meat and wine and other marvels… but there's no magic in it…

ROSS. It's just a kind of poison, isn't it?

HELEN. Yes.

The Devil came to me when I'd swallowed nothing at all… I saw him clearer then.

And the Devil has told me what I am.

HELEN *unwraps her bundle. She holds up a long-dead crow by one wing.*

I woke that morning and you'd taken my mother from me. Oh, master, I wished you dead then. I cried out in such a rage of ill-wishing then, so all the crows flew up out of the tree-tops, I cried out again, such a howl of black rage from the roots of my belly... and the birds fell from the air as my hate scorched the life out of them...

JANET. What are you saying, darling!?

HELEN. I killed them. With the power that's in me.

JANET. The air is full of ice, Helen! The birds are dropping off their branches just from breathing...

HELEN (*driving over her*). I know what I am now. I know what must happen to me. I'd rather die than live with what's in me, never knowing church or neighbours again...

So please, sir...

JANET. No...

HELEN. If you're looking for your witch, it's me. My mother's just a poor old soul. It's her pride that makes her think she's magic.

JANET. No...

HELEN. And you should burn me for the power that's in me... or else I'll be driven out soon enough.

ROSS. Well... the law says a witch may be convicted on the word of another witch... so we must say she can be pardoned by the same token...

JANET. She's no witch! I charmed her. Her head's full of moonlight and nonsense! I turned it with charms when she was still growing inside me. Look how she came out twisted!

HELEN. No!

JANET. Look at her hands! Look at her feet! I've shoed her like an ugly little pony and ridden her through the sky.

HELEN. No!

JANET. There's nothing in her head I didn't put there.

HELEN. That's not true…

JANET. Oh, that's the truth. She hasn't the wits of her father! He was dying as soon as she fell out of me. His wits went. Ask anyone, kick Douglas awake and ask him! That whole family are thick with poor creatures and slobbering idiots. You could show her a stick from the shore and she'd call it the Devil. You could pull a stone out of the ground and she'd cradle it like a bairn. Look at her! Seventeen and no one halfway human'll have her.

HELEN. You'll not let me go…

JANET. It's sorcery! My sorcery's addled her wits. She's just my vessel. Nothing more.

HELEN. She can't charm warts onto a toad…

JANET. Look at her! Do you think if she had it in her to make a witch I wouldn't teach her all I knew? She barely knows her own name! She can't even pick up peas with both hands!

HELEN. You said I should never mind that! You said… You said I was beautiful!

JANET. She's halfway to an idiot! So she's dreamed the dreams I've conjured for her and the halfwit thinks they're real! She's seen her mother call the wind to heel like a great hunting dog and now she fancies she can do the same trick herself!

HELEN. You can't call the wind!

JANET *is suddenly right at the length of her chain, right in* HELEN*'s face.*

JANET. A witch's get, too stupid to think what it means to a mother to see its bairn dead before her, killed before her eyes. How stupid is that? If she'd one speck of my wits she'd never speak so! But she hasn't the sense of a staggering calf!

She thinks death's a present she means to steal from my press, well, I'll slam the lid on your fingers, my babe. Now hold your mouth and do as you're told!

A beat.

ROSS. Well… as long as we find one witch here I'd say the law will rest happy.

A beat.

HELEN. Oh, Mother, please… please…

JANET *smiles at her, shaking her head.*

JANET. I confess myself a witch.

HELEN. No.

JANET. I renounced my baptism. I was a poor, puddled soul in cold and in hunger and the Deil came to me and said if I would have no master but him I'd never know want again. 'Well,' I says, 'That'll suit me fine. Just give me some bread and warm meat and my soul's yours for a watch fob. So he gave me a bit of bacon and a loaf of bread. Oh, it was braw. We had beer as well, warm and strong. Then I was the Devil's creature. I killed Douglas Begg's stirk and cured Mary Mackenzie's pig. I used my own daughter as my beast of burden, I rode her like a horse across the sky and she too witless to throw me off. And at last the Devil came to me in the form of a bonny young man with silver buttons on his coat. So I lay with the Devil. Three times. And his breath was cold and his cock was hot and I knew he was evil by the look in his eye when he stared down at my nakedness, hungry and terrified together. And when he came in me he cried out like a wee bairn, lost and screaming for its mother… but no mother bore him… she'd've dashed the Devil's brains out on a rock the minute she saw his twisted face and knew what was growing inside him.

A long pause. JANET *is just staring down* ROSS.

Once you've touched him, the Devil'll have your soul, one way or another, eh, Captain Ross? The best you can hope for is to cheat him of any pleasure in chewing on it.

ROSS. You confess?

JANET. Yes. I kissed the Devil's arse and he fucking loved it!

ROSS. In front of these witnesses and already accused by Douglas Begg as a known witch, you confess you have denounced your baptism and you have lain with the Devil and made your pact with him?

JANET. Oh, I've done that all right.

ROSS. Then that's all the law requires and you shall burn for it.

ROSS *and* JANET *are still just staring at each other.*

HELEN *starts to cry quietly.*

NIALL (*uncertain*). No, man... we have to wait until the Privy Council reviews the case... for a capital sentence...

HELEN. Oh, Mammy, I'm feart! I'm feart.

ROSS. If the Privy Council had any care for the folk of Dornoch and their safety from sorcery, they would have sent word before now.

I am the security of law and order here. I pass sentence and we'll act on it tomorrow. If the lawyers in Edinburgh have a problem with my justice they can chide me later.

JANET. Are we done then?

ROSS *smiles. Relaxed now. He drops her chain and steps back.*

ROSS. We're done.

The minute he steps back, JANET *hurls herself forward the length of her chain, and grabs* HELEN *in her arms.*

JANET. Oh, my clever, beautiful little bird. My clever little bird. You'll learn to fly yet. Stay safe, keep out of the storm.

HELEN *is clinging to* JANET*, crying.* NIALL *and* ROSS *pull her off.*

ROSS. Get her out of here.

NIALL *tries to pull* HELEN *away.*

JANET. Remember who you are!

HELEN turns to ROSS.

HELEN. If I have the power, I'll send a hoody crow to peck the heart out of you. You'd hear its wings in your sleep, and see its black eye watching you from every fence post and never know peace again.

ROSS. Get her out!

NIALL pulls HELEN off.

ROSS and JANET are left looking at each other.

JANET. Well, Davey, I could sleep on a bed of gravel.

She lies down and is instantly asleep.

ROSS stares at her a moment. Then he goes and kicks DOUGLAS awake.

ROSS. Get up! Get up! You've to get ready.

DOUGLAS looks round, blinking.

DOUGLAS. What is it?

Sees JANET.

Is she dead?

ROSS. Not yet, we've broken her. Get up. You've work to do.

DOUGLAS. Aye... God... aye, I'm needing back to my beasts.

ROSS. Time enough for that. You've to kill this creature tomorrow. We need a cart to carry it and the barrel it'll burn in. We'll set the fire itself in the churchyard.

DOUGLAS. We're to kill her?

ROSS. She's guilty. All the proof the law needs.

As DOUGLAS gapes at him:

You're the town locksmith. It's your office to stand as hangman or witch-burner as well.

DOUGLAS. Aye, but...

ROSS. But what?

DOUGLAS. It's never come to that so…

ROSS. It's come to that now.

DOUGLAS. We're to kill her?

ROSS. She'll be executed tomorrow…

DOUGLAS. But… she's my neighbour! I've known her nearly twenty years!

ROSS. And you know she's a witch.

What did you think was going to happen?

DOUGLAS. Well, I never thought we'd break her. She's as stubborn as a limpet.

ROSS. Is there tar to be had?

DOUGLAS. Eh?

ROSS. Tar. To burn her?

DOUGLAS. Aye… eh… Stuart Golspie might have some left from his byre roof but, eh… God… Well, he'll want paying.

ROSS (*sighs, handing him a coin*). Have the minister raise a collection to cover that.

DOUGLAS. And kindling… I mean… who's got spare kindling this time of year, you know…

ROSS (*another coin*). Buy what you need. The rest is your fee for your work.

DOUGLAS. My work… aye…

ROSS. You've never done it?

DOUGLAS. Christ, no!

ROSS. You put a barrel of tar on the cart. You put the witch in the barrel. You parade her through the streets. You take her to the burning ground and carry the barrel to the post. You tie her to the post. You put a thin rope round her neck and strangle her till there's no life in her. Then you light a fire round the tar barrel.

DOUGLAS. Aye, well... I can... I can maybe buy some wood, but...

ROSS. What?

DOUGLAS. God save me, sir! I can't strangle Janet like a chicken!

ROSS. Well, who else is to do it? It's your office.

DOUGLAS. Well... I can fetch the tar... find the kindling, but...

ROSS. She's to die. The law says that your hand's appointed to kill her.

DOUGLAS. Aye, but...

ROSS. What?

DOUGLAS. I can't! I can't strangle Janet!

ROSS. Then she'll burn alive.

DOUGLAS *just gapes at him.*

Fine. That serves me just as well. Better. Fetch the wood and tar.

ROSS *exits.*

DOUGLAS *looks at* JANET *sleeping on the floor.*

Abruptly he breaks down.

DOUGLAS. Oh God! Oh Jesus, what have I done?   regret

He goes to JANET *and cradles her, half-lifting her.*

Oh, Janet, I'm sorry. I'm sorry.

JANET (*barely waking*). Douglas, will you keep it down? I'm needing my rest.

Scene Two

Near Janet Horne's house – night.

ELSPETH *is helping* HELEN *bundle her possessions together.*

ELSPETH. Take my shawl. Here… you're shivering already.

> You cursed him! You cursed him, you say!

HELEN (*shaking*). Yes.

ELSPETH. Oh, God save us…

> Well, there's no power in it. He'll know that. He'll see that. Just a wee girl, angry he's hurting her mother.

HELEN. I'm full-grown, Elspeth.

ELSPETH. I know it.

> I know it.

> He'll know it. He'll think of it any moment. He'll likely be thinking of it now.

HELEN. What?

ELSPETH. That the witch's get should go along with her. You can't just shoot the falcon… you have to smash her eggs and burn the nest.

HELEN. I'll hide out. Up in the forest by the peats till…

ELSPETH. Helen… Helen, you can never come back. Never.

> Never in this life.

> Never till the world's end. He'll break and burn you too.

HELEN. But…

ELSPETH. You can never come back.

HELEN (*starting to cry*). But he won't kill her. He won't. How would anyone let him?

ELSPETH. It's going to happen.

HELEN. No.

ELSPETH. It's the law.

HELEN. But it's just him! Tell him to stop. Make him stop!

ELSPETH. He won't be stopped. The whole country's in terror of his law.

HELEN. You can't let him kill her!

ELSPETH. I'll go and see her dead and I'll throw a curse at her, Helen. I have to. I wouldn't accuse her. I have to curse her to stay alive. And you have to fly away. *okay elspeth!*

HELEN. I've no wings.

ELSPETH. Oh, here, chick… here… Take my bit of bread… take some cheese…

HELEN. I can't…

ELSPETH. Take a kiss from me, Helen… take a last kiss and my blessing for your journey…

She hugs HELEN.

HELEN. Oh, Elspeth, don't drive me out! Where will I go? Where can I go?

ELSPETH. Any road that turns away from Loth. Never stop walking, pet. Never stop. You must be lost for ever now.

HELEN. I don't want to be lost. I want to stay here.

ELSPETH. Take my name. Helen… listen… listen… sweetheart… This will save you. You're Elspeth Begg's wayward girl that ran off with a sailor. That's why you've nothing but the clothes on you. That's why you're lost.

You're Elspeth Begg's but she never wants to see you back again.

You know nothing of Janet Horne and her trouble. You can never go home again because of your mother's tears and your father's anger. You're a beggar living off the pity of the women with roofs over their heads. But you're alive.

HELEN. She's my mother.

ELSPETH. No.

No. You're my lost daughter and I never want to see you more.

Pulling HELEN *close again.*

Oh, God keep you safe, Helen.

Never stop walking.

ELSPETH *leaves.*

HELEN *picks up her bundle. Slowly she starts walking.*

She is stumbling on her road in the dark. Crying. She stops, hugging herself, comforting herself.

HELEN. It's all right, little bird, it's all right, you'll get through this, you'll find the road, you'll be safe... There now... there now...

She slows her breathing.

NICK *is watching her from the shadows.*

She sees him.

Why are you following me?

NICK. You know.

And you, just a thin white flower.

HELEN. You can't pick up what's not offered to you. You can't touch anything that doesn't put itself under your hand. You can't go where you're not invited.

NICK. All true.

HELEN. So go away.

She turns her back on him, pulling up her bundle to walk on.

NICK. You don't want me to go away.

HELEN. I do.

NICK. You did before. Now, now you want to ask me a favour.

HELEN. No.

NICK. Ask me.

HELEN. I'll eat stones first.

NICK. Ask me. Ask me!

A beat.

HELEN *turns and looks at him.*

HELEN. And what do you get… for my asking?

They're making a bargain.

NICK. You'll follow me.

HELEN. I'll not.

NICK. Then I'll still follow you.

HELEN. You'll never catch me.

NICK. Well… we'll see about that. I've caught quicker birds than you.

HELEN. If you do I'll be gone before you wake.

NICK. Then I'll be hard behind you a blink later.

HELEN. All my days?

NICK. All the roads you ever walk.

Will you make the bargain with me?

A beat.

HELEN. Yes.

NICK. So ask me.

HELEN. Save her.

NICK. She's held in iron. I can't.

HELEN (*breaking down*). Oh God, then just take the pain from her! Take the pain from her!

NICK. It's done.

NICK*'s gone.*

HELEN *stands alone on the road.*

Scene Three

Near the cathedral in Dornoch.

A stake has been placed where the marks of the old fire were.

JANET *has been placed before it, up to her waist in a barrel of tar.*

NIALL *and* ROSS *are standing looking at her,* DOUGLAS *close by.*

NIALL. Can you not do it?

ROSS. I can't lay my hands on her. The law forbids it. Only the court-appointed executioner.

NIALL. To burn her alive… It's too cruel.

ROSS. She's kissed the Devil. She'll be burning till the end of time. Might as well make an early start.

I've paid a tink to light the fire.

DOUGLAS *starts to tie* JANET *to the stake. He's shaking. He's in bits.*

ELSPETH *is on, watching.*

DOUGLAS. You all right there, Janet…? Just, eh… just put your hands round behind for me, will you?

ELSPETH (*shouting across*). I'll see you burn for what you've brought to me and mine, Janet Horne.

DOUGLAS. Now, tell me if this is too tight.

JANET. Oh, hurry up, will you? Look at the state of you, your hands are shaking like the minister spying through the privy door.

ELSPETH. May everything that's yours be lost! May everything you ever loved grow wings and fly away for ever and ever! May you never see it more in this world or the one before you!

It's gone from you, Janet Horne! Do you hear me, witch!? Your dearest treasure's flown away now!

JANET (*understanding*). I hear you.

You fat hen.

DOUGLAS *has tied her. He steps away. He stands with his back to the execution and doesn't watch any of it.*

ELSPETH. Aye, and I'll watch you burn, Janet Horne. Hear me? I'll stay to the end of you.

JANET. You do that. Much joy may it bring you, you...

She can't go on.

(*Quiet, to herself.*) I hear you, Elspeth, I hear you...

ROSS *walks over to stand close to* JANET.

ROSS. Did you see this? In my hand?

JANET. You know I did. You know I see all the way into your soul.

ROSS. Then you should've feared me. Shouldn't you, Janet? You see the anger in me now? You see the red beast?

JANET. I saw the end of your days. Shall I tell you how you die, Captain Ross?

ROSS *hesitates.*

Oh, he's tempted. Spare me the fire and I'll tell you all, Davey.

(*Wobbling.*) Oh, spare me yet.

ROSS. I'll spare you nothing.

 NICK *comes on with a torch and a tinderbox.*

 Here's the fire that'll burn you, Janet Horne. What do you say?

JANET (*terror, defiance*). I say…

 I say, it's a cold day. It'll be a bonny warming.

 And that's all I'll tell you. So murder me.

 ROSS *walks back.* NICK *is already striking flint, trying to raise a flame to light the torch.*

 (*To* NICK.) Well, look at you. Aren't you a bonny young thing, come to kill me.

NICK. So it seems.

JANET. Is your flint damp there, laddie? If they'd cut me down I could get a spark out of you.

NICK. I doubt not but you could.

JANET. Oh, I can light a fire in the coldest heart, laddie, that's what's killed me…

 (*Starting to lose it.*) Oh Jesus… they're killing me… they're killing me… they're…

 NICK *has got his torch lit. He speaks close to* JANET.

NICK. I can walk through smoke and flame. Don't be frightened. I'll come for you, sweetheart.

 NICK *lights the fire.*

 ELSPETH *is shouting at* JANET *again. This is comfort disguised as cursing.*

ELSPETH. I'm watching you, you black-hearted whore!

JANET. And I'm looking back, Elspeth Begg!

ELSPETH. I'll keep my eyes on you till you're dead!

JANET. I'll remember your face in hell, you bag of farts!

ELSPETH. Keep your eyes on me, Janet Horne.

JANET. I will.

ELSPETH. Keep looking at me, you… cow… you…

(*Fighting tears.*) You… thing, you…

JANET. I see you. I see your big useless moonface, you…

(*Faltering.*) Oh, sweetheart… Elspeth…

(*Catching herself.*) Everything you're wishing on me back at you! All you deserve will come to you, Elspeth Begg! All!

And then there's just a great flash of fire and smoke as all the tar ignites at once.

Nothing is visible through the flame but JANET.

She cries out in pain and terror.

Then NICK *steps through the flames to stand close beside her. He leans into her.*

NICK. I'm here, darling. I'm here.

This for your bonny daughter's sake.

He takes out HELEN's *little silver knife and holds it high.*

JANET *sees it.*

JANET. Oh, God bless you!

He stabs her dead.

The fire covers everything.

Scene Four

High on the hill, looking back into town.

HELEN. Oh, see it…

See the smoke.

Rising in the air like a swarm of bees. There's a wind coming. A warm wind out of the south. You can smell the honey on it… It'll blow the ice out of the air. Turn all the frozen ground soft with water. One warm day to keep us breathing till the sun is fat and yellow again. I'm calling it… Blow that reek over the silver sea. I remember. I remember. My mother could charm the fish out of those waves. She could. Here comes the wind.

A warm gust. HELEN *raises her face to it a moment.*

(*Watching.*) Look at the dark smoke, blown like a veil over all the fields and woods and water…

Quicker than any bird of the air.

HELEN *watches the fire far below a moment more.*

The Devil's close behind me, Mother. I can't ever stop now.

HELEN *raises her bundle and walks off.*

Scene Five

Near the cathedral in Dornoch.

The execution site. There is nothing left but smoking charcoal. NICK *is raking through the ashes, breaking bones to bits with a cudgel.*

Only ROSS *is left, still watching.*

NICK. All the bits of her in a sack and then that in the river. Is that how you're wanting it, master?

ROSS. Yes.

NICK (*poking about*). Not even an extra bit of silver left on her finger bones.

ROSS (*sharp*). Leave that! Just break her bones.

NICK. I just thought to save you an extra coin for my work.

ROSS. You've been paid.

ROSS *is seeing something close by. He hisses, waving his stick at it.*

NICK. You'll not pay me for this extra work?

ROSS. You've been paid all you'll get, now finish it or I'll have you chased out of town.

NICK. But then you'll owe me, master, and what will we do about that?

ROSS. I don't owe you one more piece of copper. Keep working.

NICK. Need to take something for my trouble...

ROSS *isn't listening, stamping, claps his hands...*

What are you about there?

ROSS. Crows. Hoody crows on the church wall. We need to scare them off.

NICK. Do we?

They'll not hurt you, master. They just smelt the burning meat. They'll stay while the reek's in the air.

Why would they stay longer?

ROSS *claps and stamps again.*

Aye.

A cruel death, you might say, but I've seen worse.

Can you imagine, master… can you imagine what it would be like to feel a sickness in you? To know death was coming for you. To see it watching you every day and know it was going to wither you before you were ever old. Take your strength before you'd ever grown into it. Chew you down to nothing but bones before you'd even scratched a mark on the earth that's just waiting to bury you. The idea of that would just take a man's peace of mind altogether, wouldn't it? And who can put a price on a man's peace of mind? That's worth more than rubies.

NICK *has finished scraping ash into a sack. He stands watching* ROSS.

ROSS *is still scaring crows.*

See that one flying back to the same stone every time?

(*Laughs*.) He's sure there's a meal for him somewhere, eh?

ROSS *notices* NICK *again.*

ROSS. Are you done?

NICK. Unless you've anything else for me.

ROSS. Take that rubbish away with you and don't let me see you begging round here more.

NICK. That's fine, master.

I've everything I'm wanting.

I've a long road to walk, but I doubt not I'll see you again one day.

NICK *exits, carrying the sack.*

ROSS *is looking at the crows.*

He hisses, trying to scare them again.

We hear the cawing, then the sound of wings, growing louder and louder.

ROSS *waves his stick in the air.*

The cawing is rising to a crescendo.

The beating of a hundred black wings. Filling the air.

Hiding ROSS *from sight.*

The End.